Preserving Beautiful Purity with

Good Character for the Next Generation

_____

Published in the United States by GOOD CHARACTER MISSION,
an imprint of the Good Character Mission Inc.
www.goodtreemission.com

First published in 2024 (print edition)

Originally published in Korean, 좋아성 : 좋은 성품으로 지키는 아름다운 성,
published in 2023 by LYS Goodtree Character School.
Copyright © 2023 by Young Suk Lee, Ph.D.

ISBN 978-1-7358273-2-2
eBook ISBN 978-1-7358273-3-9

Good Character
Sex Education

Author Young Suk Lee, Ph.D.
Translation Hee Jong Kim, Ph.D.
Illustration You Jong Kim

GOOD CHARACTER MISSION

Recommendation

For a long time, we have believed that God determines gender. However, recently, there has been a notion that gender is something one can choose. Consequently, a 'third gender,' neither male nor female, has emerged. This has led to confusion even in something as basic as using the restroom.

According to the Bible, all these phenomena are merely signs of the end times. We are experiencing the relativization of values in the postmodern era. The issue is how to protect our children from these societal upheavals. It is about raising our children within the excellent plan of creation.

Goodtree Character School is a gift from heaven. Through the beautiful character taught at Goodtree Character School, we can dream of restoring the original beautiful nature of gender. This dream fosters hope for the restoration of lovely families. I eagerly anticipate the good fruits borne by the noble men and women nurtured by the Goodtree.

Sons and daughters as initially envisioned by God! Do not conform to the world, but stand as those who change it! Let men be men and women be women. You are the light of the world, the only hope in history!

Rev. Dong Won Lee
Director of Global Pastoral Leadership Center

Introduction

California's Child Gender Transition Protection Act SB 107 and a Father's Heartfelt Cry

In January 2023, we heard the heartbreaking cry of a father in California, USA. It is the story of Jeff Younger, a father of twins from Texas. This father's poignant plea began when his ex-wife wanted to raise their twin son, James, as a girl. From age two, the mother dressed him in dresses and called him by the female name, Luna. While with his father, James was his natural self, a boy, but with his mother, he became a girl. Teachers at school also followed the mother's demands, dressing James in girls' clothes and instructing him to use the girls' bathroom even if he tried to use the boys' bathroom.

Eventually, the mother moved to Los Angeles with ten-year-old James to transition him. The 'California Child Gender Transition Protection Act SB 107,' which came into effect on January 1, 2023, provided a legal means to make James permanently 'Luna' through chemical castration and hormone treatment. Despite the father's plea, "I just want to raise my son as a boy," the world did not stand by his side. In the end, this horrific event altered the natural gender identity of a young boy at the hands of his family, school, and society.

Global Trends in Sex Education and the Inclusion of Sexuality

At some point, the illogical notion that 'one can choose one's gender' became an international issue, transforming into policies and spreading as a cultural norm. The refusal to acknowledge one's innate biological gender has given rise to so-called 'transgender rights laws,' creating significant confusion about gender identity among the next generation.

These attempts act as destructive weapons that undermine the order and laws of life as created by God. Even more disturbing is that UNESCO, the United Nations agency specializing in education and culture, promotes this 'Comprehensive Sexuality Education (CSE)' as part of the 'Global Education 2030' agenda, spreading it as the global trend in sex education.

The sex education that our children currently receive in public education follows UNESCO's 2018 revised edition of the "International Technical Guidance on Sexuality Education." This guide is so comprehensive that it is often called the 'International Standard for Sex Education,' providing detailed, age-appropriate education through a gradual, continuous, and inclusive spiral curriculum.

The controversy lies in the content. UNESCO's sex education guide explicitly states that the curriculum's foundation is Comprehensive Sexuality Education (CSE), which covers the cognitive, emotional, physical, and social aspects of sexuality. Parents exposed to this education have continually reported to the international community that it 'sexualizes children from ages 5 to 18.'

Pro-homosexual stance and teaching abortion as 'human rights': How can this become the mainstream in sex education? Criticism and research with adverse outcomes continue to follow the teaching of a pro-homosexual stance and abortion as 'human rights' as part of sex education. Should we unconditionally accept UNESCO's sex education simply because it is considered an international standard and global trend and remain silent about this education?

Creative Countermeasures to Comprehensive Sexuality Education (CSE): Good Character Sex Education (GCSE)

This book is the result of such contemplation. Teaching that one can ignore biological sex and choose their gender, using sexuality as a human right to discuss feminism, legalizing abortion, and enacting homosexual laws are aspects of misguided sex education that destroy life, undermine the intrinsic value of humanity, and lead to the tragic loss of God's image.

The most precious value that the next generation should learn through sexuality is to reflect the image of God, who created us. Teaching the beautiful values of sexuality from the unchanging and precious truth of the Bible is the true sex education that parents and teachers must impart.

The author has reviewed and organized 'Biblical Sexual Values' to replace the five key aspects of UNESCO's sex education—gender sensitivity, gender identity education, gender equality, consent education, and sexuality—both educationally and culturally.

Thus, we have included educational content and methodologies to foster 'Creationist Sensitivity, Self-identity Education, Sexual Responsibility, Obedience Education, and Biblical Sexual Truth.' These strategies are designed to save and restore life.

Each topic presents the characteristics of our Creator God as good qualities to learn, structured into a curriculum called 'GCSE (Protecting the beauty of sex through good character)' Each unit includes beautiful character songs and storytelling from Goodtree Character School, cultivated over the past 19 years, making sex education fun and joyful.

As time passes, we feel the truth is God's 'Omnipotence and Greatness.' Just as God's passion for loving the next generation prepares the early and latter rains, we are grateful for the Lord's hand in continuing Goodtree Character School's 12 Character Education, prepared since 2005, as life-saving sex education for the next generation.

Through 'GCSE (Protecting the beauty of sex through good character),' we pray that parents and teachers of this era can confidently spread 'Biblical Sexual Education' worldwide.

August 2024.

Young Suk Lee, Ph.D

Contents

Do Not Imitate This Generation

Goodtree Character School

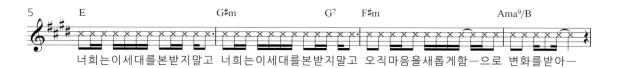

How to Use This Book

"GCSE: Protecting the beauty of sex through good character" is designed with a Christian worldview for parents and teacher to first learn and internalize to establish the correct 'Biblical sexual values' for the next generation.

Implement in **Churches** as a 5-Week Course!

Operate 'GCSE (Good Character Sex Education)' to protect the next generation's lives.

Teach at **Home!**

Parents, teach your children GCSE to protect them from the world.

Implement as a Sex Education Curriculum in Christian Alternative **Schools**!

The most urgent GCSE (Good Character Sex Education) to save the next generation! Establish through GCSE.

Structure of GCSE:

Story Telling	Doing & Being	Let's Study	Building Bridges
It helps to form cognitive concepts of GCSE. (Cognitive Domain)	It helps to apply what is learned in GCSE storytelling to daily life. (Behavioral Domain)	It helps to explore GCSE more deeply from the perspective of a creative worldview. (Scientific, Logical Thinking Extension Domain)	It helps to accept GCSE educational content with positive emotions, leading to cognitive expansion. (Emotional Domain)

* **Theme Character Traits:** Learn the Korean and English definitions of each lesson's theme character trait through songs via QR codes.

* **Scripture to Protect Me:** Memorize the theme scripture of each lesson.

* **Character Songs:** Joyfully learn the theme character traits of each lesson through songs.

* **GCSE Stories:** Parents and teachers must first understand the core themes of each chapter to prepare for teaching the next generation.

* **GCSE Counseling Q&A:** This resource helps parents and teachers provide the correct biblical answers when the next generation asks questions about sexuality.

* **GCSE Workbook :** Separate age-specific GCSE workbooks for practical educational activities (Story Telling, Doing & Being, Let's Study, Building Bridges).

Chapter 1

Biblical Sensitivity

Creativity

Stage 1 Trying and trying and trying new ways.

Creativity means "coming up with exciting ideas and trying something new."

Stage 2 Trying different ways with new ideas.

Caring

Stage 1 Observing others and helping them be happy.

Stage 2 Giving love and attention to the world around me.

Chapter 1 Did You Know?

Creativity : Trying different ways with new ideas.

In the beginning God created the heavens and the earth.
(Genesis 1:1)

Chapter 2 Look, Look

Caring : Giving love and attention to the world around me.

God blessed them and said to them, "Be fruitful and increase in number; fill the earth and subdue it. Rule over the fish of the sea and the birds of the air and over every living creature that moves on the ground." (Genesis 1:28)

Did You Know?

Did you know?
Do you know who made it?

The bright shining day,
The dark and gloomy night,
Who made them?

Look over there! That's the sky,
And this is the sea.
Who made them?

The pretty rose, the tall tree,
Who made the delicious grapes?

The blazing sun, the soft moon,
Who made the twinkling stars?

Look for the Milky Way and the Big Dipper,
Can you see them?

The beautiful birds flying in the sky,
The fish swimming in the water,
Isn't it amazing?
Who made them?

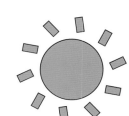

The giraffe with a long neck,
the elephant with a long trunk,
Who made them?

But, you know, there is an even
more special creation:
Man and woman!

He made man and woman and
was especially pleased!

Because they resemble the
Creator, God.

He entrusted all the beautiful things in this
world to them,
"Be fruitful and increase in number! Fill the
earth!"

Aha, that's why you and I are here,
In the likeness of God!

Say it out loud,
The world that God made,
It's truly wonderful!

Look, Look

Look, look,
Just like you and me,
God created man and woman.

Oh, the chickens? Hen and rooster!
That's why they lay white eggs.

Because there are daddy chickens and
mommy chickens,
Little chicks can be born peeping.

Look, look,
Just like you and me,
God created man and woman.

Oh, a lion?
Female and male!
Really? How can you tell?

Aha, you can tell by looking at this.
Female and male!

Look, look,
Just like you and me,
God created man and woman.

Do pretty flowers also have male and female,
Just like you and me?

Aha, they do! They do!
Even flowers that don't move have male and
female.
This is the pistil, and that is the stamen.

Aha, that's how they bear fruit.
The whole world is made that way.

Just like you and me, man and
woman!
God created us.

But why did He create us?
For you, and for me,

To love each other,
To be thankful for each other,
To take care of each other.

Chapter 2

Understanding
My Identity

Joyfulness

Stage 1 I am precious. You are precious. So we are happy.

Stage 2 Always having a happy heart without complaints

Positive Attitude

Stage 1 Thinking, acting, and speaking in a good way.

Stage 2 Always choosing to have the best thoughts about
something or someone

Chapter 3 **Who Are You?**

Joyfulness : I am precious. You are precious. So we are happy.

———

So God created man in his own image, in the image of God he created him; male and female he created them.(Genesis 1:27)

Chapter 4 **The Hidden Treasure Within Me**

Positive Attitude : Thinking, acting, and speaking in a good way.

———

For we are God's workmanship, created in Christ Jesus to do good works, which God prepared in advance for us to do. (Ephesians 2:10)

Who Are You?

Your eyes are black and round,
Your face is round like a ball,
Your hair is curly and soft.

Oh! You and I are similar but different.

Who are you?
Aha, you are a boy!

Who am I, with white and round
features?

My hands are pretty,
And I walk gracefully,
So beautiful, like a princess.

Who are you?
Aha, you are a girl!

You and I,
Though we look different, we are all
God's creations.

You and I,
Though we look different, we are all
God's creations.

You are so precious,
I am so precious,

Just as we are,
Rejoicing in the way God made us,
I am a child of joy.

The Hidden Treasure Within Me

People say I look like a boy,
But I am a girl.
The secret of my birth:
"XX"
I don't change.

People say I look like a girl,
But I am a boy.
The secret of my birth:
"XY"
I don't change.

People say I look like OO,
But in fact, I am a "treasure."
My value doesn't change.

According to the plan of the One who created me long
ago, my value never changes.

I am "hope," crafted according to God's plan.
I am "promise," formed by the love of my mom and dad.
I am a "positive OO," growing with good thoughts, feelings,
and actions on this earth.

Chapter 3

Learning My Sexual Responsibility

CHARACTER THEMES

Honesty

Stage 1 Lies? No! Truth? Yes!
Honesty means "expressing things as they are."

Stage 2 Winning the trust of others by always telling the truth.

Responsibility

Stage 1 Doing your best all the time.
Stage 2 Knowing what my tasks are and doing them the best I can.

Chapter 5 **Marriage Is Precious**

Honesty : Winning the trust of others by always telling the truth.

———

For this reason a man will leave his father and mother and be united to his wife, and they will become one flesh. (Genesis 2:24)

Chapter 6 **Men are Fathers, Women are Mothers!**

Responsibility : Knowing what my tasks are and doing them the best I can.

———

Marry and have sons and daughters; find wives for your sons and give your daughters in marriage, so that they too may have sons and daughters. Increase in number there; do not decrease. (Jeremiah 29:6)

Marriage Is Precious

Speak honestly.
Based on your feelings, you cannot decide whether you are a man or a woman.
Speak honestly about whether you are a man or a woman, just as the Creator God has chosen us to be and as you were born.

Honesty means "winning the trust of others by always telling the truth in thought, word, and action, no matter the situation."
You cannot decide based on feelings.
Honestly, as you were born:
I am a man; you are a woman.

Speak honestly.
Marriage is formed when one man and one woman come together.
What does that mean?
It means a woman and a man get married.
That is why marriage is precious.

Speak honestly.
When one man and woman come together and love each other, the most beautiful 'baby' in the world is born.

That's how I was born, and that's how my sibling was born.
That is why marriage is precious.

Speak honestly.
How is a baby born?

The baby seed inside a man is called 'sperm.'
The baby seed inside a woman is called an 'egg.'
A baby is made when the sperm and egg meet.
One man becomes a father, one woman becomes a mother,
And that is why marriage is precious.

Speak honestly.
What is a 'family'?
A family is when one woman, who has become a mother, and one man, who has become a father, protect us responsibly. That is what a 'family' is.

A beautiful family is where we are lovingly cared for until we grow up and become adults.

Speak honestly.
Marriage is between one man and one woman.

Men are Fathers, Women are Mothers!

The little prince grew up to become a
wonderful man,
And finally became a dad.
The little princess grew up to become a
beautiful woman,
And finally became a mom.

Men are dads, Women are moms!

Even though what they do may be
different, their love for us is the
same.

It's called "responsibility."
I know my tasks and do them the
best I can until the end.

With the character trait of
responsibility,
They love us.

Mom carefully protected me when I was in her belly.

Dad protected Mom and me so that I could be born healthy.

I love it most when I snuggle in Mom's arms.
I have the most fun when I play with Dad.

By watching Mom and Dad love each other, we learn how to love.
Mom and Dad's love helps us grow strong and healthy.

Someday, I will also become a mom or dad.
And live with love.

Chapter 4

Protecting Myself Through Obedience

Patience

Stage 1 Waiting until good things happen.

Stage 2 Waiting in peace for a good thing to happen.

Obedience

Stage 1 Happily doing what my parents say.

Stage 2 Following the instructions of others with a good attitude.

Goodtree Character School Definition | Copyright No. C-2014-008458 | US Copyright No. TX 8-721-576

Chapter 7 We Need to Wait

Patience : Waiting in peace for a good thing to happen.
Goodtree Character School Definition | Copyright No. C-2014-008458 | US Copyright No. TX 8-721-576

_____

Perseverance must finish its work so that you may be
mature and complete, not lacking anything. (James 1:4)

Chapter 8 The Secret to
Protecting Myself

Obedience : Following the instructions of others with a
good attitude.
Goodtree Character School Definition | Copyright No. C-2014-008458 | US Copyright No. TX 8-721-576

_____

Children, obey your parents in everything, for this pleases
the Lord. (Colossians 3:20)

We Need to Wait

There is a time for everything.
Just like delicious apples wait through spring,
summer, and fall to ripen in the sunlight.

A baby is born, crawls around,
Then stands up and runs,
Becomes a brave student like an older sibling
and eventually a wonderful adult.
You have to wait for all these stages.

As your body and mind grow,
You must also wait for a man and a woman to meet and marry.

You need to wait for your growth patiently,
Because sexuality is beautiful and marriage is precious.

Patience means waiting in
peace for a good thing to
happen.

With the character trait of patience,
We wait for that beautiful time.

The Secret to Protecting Myself

The most precious "me" in this world,
How do I protect myself?

Is it my body, so can I do whatever I want?
NO, NO! That's not okay.
Can I do whatever I desire?
NO, NO! That's not okay.

The secret to protecting myself is growing up
obedient to God, who created me and knows
everything about me.

The secret to protecting myself is growing up in
obedience to my mom, dad, and
teachers,
Who love me the most and know
me the best in this world.

Obedience is following the instructions of others with a good attitude.

For my beautiful growth,
For my bright future,
I protect myself with the character trait of obedience.

Until my body grows bigger and stronger,

Until my heart grows deeper and more beautiful.

Chapter 5

Discern the World Through Biblical Sexual Truth

CHARACTER THEMES

Self-Control

Stage 1 When I want to do things my way, stop and behave.

Stage 2 Choosing to do what is right even if it's not what I want.

Wisdom

Stage 1 Helping others with what I know.
Wisdom means "doing things that bring joy to yourself and others."

Stage 2 Using what I have and what I know to help others.

Chapter 9　The One Who
　　　　　Overcomes the World

Self-Control : Choosing to do what is right even if it's not what I want.

Goodtree Character School Definition | Copyright No. C-2014-008458 | US Copyright No. TX 8-721-576

———

All Scripture is God-breathed and is useful for teaching, rebuking, correcting and training in righteousness, so that the man of God may be thoroughly equipped for every good work. (2 Timothy 3:16~17)

Chapter 10　True Wisdom

Wisdom : Using what I have and what I know to help others.

Goodtree Character School Definition | Copyright No. C-2014-008458 | US Copyright No. TX 8-721-576

———

Above all else, guard your heart, for it is the wellspring of life.
(Proverbs 4:23)

The One Who Overcomes the World

People say,
"If it's fun, you can do anything."
No, no!

People say,
"Your body is yours, so you can do
whatever you want."
No, no!

The things people like,
The things people want to do,
The way people think they should do things,
They call it 'culture.'

But they also call sexuality a culture.
They say, "You can do whatever you want with
'sexual culture.'"
They say, "You can do whatever you desire
with 'sexual culture.'"
They say, "You can do whatever you please
with 'sexual culture.'"
No, no!

Acting according to my desires and living based on what feels good is foolish.

Protect yourself with good character,
With the character trait of 'self-control'!
Self-control means 'choosing to do what is right even if it's not what I want.'
This is the truth.

A person who protects beautiful 'sexuality' with good character,
is the one who overcomes the world.
I will protect myself.

Protecting 'beautiful sexuality' with the character trait of self-control!
I will become the one who overcomes the world.

True Wisdom

Is this real?
Is that real?

You can't tell just by looking with your eyes.
Something that looks good might have evil
in it when you look closely.
That's why we need the ability to discern
what is real.
This is the character trait of 'wisdom.'

Wisdom is
'using what I have and what I know to help
others.'

One person says this, and another person
says that.
But there is an unchanging truth.
That is 'the truth.'

Truth is 'the right path that saves life.'
Something that remains unchanged
over time,
That is the real thing!
That is 'the truth.'

Truth helps us live rightly and
wonderfully,
It saves us and makes us happier.

How can we find that 'truth'?
Truth is found in the 'Bible,'
The story of God who created us!
The Bible teaches us to live and be
happier.

Living according to the truth learned from
the Bible is true wisdom!

To protect beautiful sexuality,
We live discerningly according to the
words of the 'Bible'!
Living according to the truth is true
'wisdom.'

Chapter 6

GCSE Stories for Parents and Teachers

Parents and Teachers Learn First!

Biblical Sensitivity
Parents and Teachers Learn First!

What image comes to mind when you think of 'sex'?

There was an incident while teaching a character at a high school in South Korea. As soon as the word 'character' (*seong poom*) was mentioned, a male student quickly raised his hand and asked, "What is character (성품, *seong poom*)? Sex toys (*seong in yong poom*)?" The classroom erupted in laughter at the student's mischievous question. This playful incident has become a frequently shared story among the instructors of the Korea Character Association, perhaps because it's pretty refreshing to see how teenagers immediately associate 'character (성품, *seong poom*)' with 'sex (성, *seong*)'.

"What image comes to mind when you think of 'sex'?"

This is a significant question for parents and teachers who are starting to teach biblical sexual values through the 'GCSE (Protecting the beauty of sex through good character). Many parents and teachers are unsure when and how to 'begin' sex education. Often, the vague goal of sex education is seen as living life enjoying oneself or ensuring that children grow into adults without any accidents or issues.

However, like any education that aims to create an excellent life, 'GCSE' has a clear 'beginning' and 'end.'

What Is Biblical Sensitivity?

The first unit of 'GCSE' starts with associating 'sex' with God. It involves cultivating 'Creation Sensitivity' to discover the good character of God the Father, who created biological sex.

According to Goodtree Character School, Creation Sensitivity is "the ability to sensitively find and recognize elements of creation in daily life."

The more you understand sex, the more you realize it is filled with God's wisdom and wit. In the world-renowned book Fearfully and Wonderfully Made (1980)[1] by Dr. Paul Brand and Philip Yancey, Dr. Paul Brand, a surgeon, marvels at life and sexuality:

"There are many things in the world that we should marvel at, but we should be most amazed by the birth of life. The birth of a human being is a miracle of miracles and a mystery of mysteries. Think about it. From the meeting of a sperm and an egg, a single fertilized cell eventually becomes 10 trillion cells, and finally, a life is born. A baby is born! How can we describe this mystery?"

Dangerous Approaches to Sex: Gender Sensitivity Education

In contrast, in modern society, the concept of sex is strangely distanced from 'life'. Instead, it is often closer to 'greed' or 'violence', which is concerning. We see the emergence of awkward terms like PGP (Preferred Gender Pronouns), where individuals choose their gender pronouns, and provocative issues that consume sexuality, confusing the identity of the next generation.

Moreover, UNESCO's International Technical Guidance on Sexuality Education explains using concepts like 'Gender' and 'Sexuality' that sex can change socially and culturally. It teaches that respecting these changes comprehensively is an unbiased and fair attitude.[2]

In particular, starting from the age of 5, children are taught about 'unequal treatment based on gender.' By 9 to 12, they learn to 'question the fairness of gender roles and challenge unjust practices.'[3] This is so-called 'gender sensitivity education.' Gender sensitivity is the sensitivity to detect elements of gender discrimination[4] in daily life. It makes individuals recall instances where they have felt discriminated against based on their gender and role.

The problem lies in enforcing this gender sensitivity education top-down rather than as a reactive approach. Instead of voluntarily educating those students who need help, it makes them first think of discrimination or imbalances they have faced due to their gender when they think about 'sex.' The fact that many young people in Korea now cry out against misogyny and misandry and engage in unproductive debates is likely not unrelated to the past 20 years of gender sensitivity education.[5]

It's Time to Respond

'GCSE (Protecting the beauty of sex through good character)' is an education that teaches God's character through biological sex. Instead of 'gender sensitivity,' it promotes 'creation sensitivity,' making students feel and experience the world of the Creator sensitively.

In Lesson 1 of 'GCSE (Protecting the beauty of sex through good character),' the next generation is brought to the great moment of creation. Through the story 'Did You Know?', they imagine the scene when God created 'sex' in the beginning. Goodtree Character School defines creativity as "trying different ways with new ideas." Through the activities of 'GCSE (Protecting the beauty of sex through good character),' students explore the delicate creativity of God, who created biological sex.

In Lesson 2 of GCSE (Protecting the beauty of sex through good character), through the story 'Look,

Look,' children learn about the beautiful plan of life that can be understood through sexuality. Goodtree Character School defines Caring as "giving love and attention to the world around me." This is a time to sensitively perceive the character of the Creator, who made sexuality with love and order.

Now, it is time for parents and teachers to respond. The 'end' of GCSE (Protecting the beauty of sex through good character) is to build the next generation who has life, and has it to the full (John 10:10). Let's start the powerful journey of life-saving sex education and learning the good character of the Creator through GCSE!

1) Fearfully and Wonderfully Made is co-authored by Dr. Paul Brand, a Christian surgeon who received the Albert Lasker Award for Basic Medical Research (often referred to as the Nobel Prize in medicine), and Philip Yancey, one of the most influential evangelical writers of our time. This book is also famous for winning the Gold Medallion Book Award from the Evangelical Christian Publishers Association (ECPA).

2) Let's confirm the three concepts of sex taught to the next generation. First, 'sex' refers to the biological aspect of gender, distinguishing between male and female. Second, 'gender' is the social aspect of sex, which considers that gender is not fixed and can change based on social situations. Third, 'sexuality' is the cultural aspect of sex, which views all sexual behaviors as subjective choices and experiences by individuals and society. The perspectives of 'gender' and 'sexuality,' particularly, stand in opposition to the biblical sexual values that distinguish sex as male and female.

3) UNESCO's International Technical Guidance on Sexuality Education 2018 revised edition, p.51, 'Gender Equality, Stereotypes and Bias.'

4) 2023 Guide for Managing and Responding to Sexual Behaviors of Young Children published by the Ministry of Health and Welfare and the Central Childcare Support Center, p.112.

5) According to the Korean Institute for Gender Equality Promotion and Education (https://eqgender.kigepe.or.kr), gender sensitivity education has been actively encouraged in all policies and programs since the 4th World Conference on Women (1995). In South Korea, gender sensitivity education was institutionalized with the addition of the 'Education for Policy Analysis and Evaluation' clause (Article 7 of the Enforcement Decree) in the Basic Women's Development Act in 2003.

■ Core Themes for Parents and Teachers

Gender Sensitivity
(Gender Sensitivity Education)

Gender sensitivity education aims to cultivate 'gender sensitivity,' the sensitivity to detect elements of gender discrimination in daily life. It is an education that understands each other's diversity and aims to realize a society where everyone is respected and treated equally.

Biblical Sensitivity

Biblical sensitivity education cultivates the sensitivity to find the truths of the creationist worldview in daily life. Contrary to the gender sensitivity taught by the world, it involves finding the creative principles of the Creator in everyday life and discovering the grand plan and mission hidden in our wonderfully created bodies and genders, striving to emulate the character of the Creator.

■ Terminology for the Next Generation

Biblical Sensitivity:
Finding the plan of being created as male and female in the world made by God.

■ Learning <Biblical Sensitivity> through Good Character

Chapter 1 — Did You Know?

창의성이란? (Korean)
모든 생각과 행동을 새로운 방법으로 시도해 보는 것

What is Creativity?
Trying different ways with new ideas.

Chapter 2 — Look, Look

배려란? (Korean)
나와 다른 사람 그리고 환경에 대하여 사랑과 관심을 갖고 잘 관찰하여 보살펴 주는 것

What is Caring?
Giving love and attention to the world around me.

Goodtree Character School Definition | Copyright No. C-2014-008458 | US Copyright No. TX 8-721-576

Overview of Good Character Sex Education Plan

	Lesson 1 Did You Know?	Lesson 2 Look, Look
GCSE Themes	Creativity Trying different ways with new ideas.	Caring Giving love and attention to the world around me.
GCSE Goals	1. Understand the 'Creator' who created the world righteously and the 'Order of Creation.' 2. Realize that 'sex' was created with the character of the Creator.	1. Learn the principles of how the whole world was created as male and female and observe the order of sex in the surroundings. 2. Develop sensitivity to find the hidden plan of life within our bodies and genders. 3. Value and care for oneself, others, and the environment with Biblical Sensitivity.
Bible Scriptures	"In the beginning, God created the heavens and the earth." (Genesis 1:1)	God blessed them and said to them, "Be fruitful and increase in number; fill the earth and subdue it. Rule over the fish of the sea and the birds of the air and over every living creature that moves on the ground." (Genesis 1:28)
Character Songs	♫ I Am God's Greatest Masterpiece (included in Goodtree Character School Jesus Caby)	♫ I Choose To Be Considerate (included in Goodtree Character School Jesus Caby)
GCSE Activity Names	• **Story Telling** Did You Know? • **Doing & Being** Who Made It? • **Let's Study** How Was It Made? • **Building Bridges** Let's Pray Together	• **Story Telling** Look, Look • **Doing & Being** Who Is My Partner? • **Let's Study** The Order of Creation Hidden in Nature • **Building Bridges** Let's Pray Together

* Note: The practical educational activities mentioned above are produced separately in age-specific GCSE workbooks.

"Wow! It was very good!"

God's exclamations began from the first day of creating the world. Each day of creation was truly perfect in itself. God made the world beautiful and abundant, reflecting His excellent nature. There was no haphazard creation of anything in the heavens, the earth, or the sea. However, there was one moment when God's creation paused with an exclamation. "Oh, this is not good!" It was when man was alone (Genesis 2:18). Finally, God created woman and called her the "Ezer kenegdo (helper suitable for him)," blessing and loving both man and woman. Only then was everything in heaven and earth completed (Genesis 2:1). Ultimately, women filled the final gap. Through the creation of gender, the world was complete.

Personal Identity Across the World
The gender-fluid trend

Meanwhile, UNESCO released the International Guidelines on Sexuality Education in 2009, with a revised edition in 2018, promoting systematic sexuality education globally, including in the United States and Korea. It's concerning that gender education[6] starts as early as age 5. The UNESCO guidelines aim to define gender and biological sex and explain their differences, particularly as a core objective of sexuality education for ages 5~8 (UNESCO International Guidelines on Sexuality Education).[7]

The emphasis on rejecting biological sex early on and choosing one's own identity is exerting a powerful influence, extending even into the fashion industry as a trend. Brands proclaiming slogans like "Reborn in Personal Fashion" are promoting concepts such as genderless[8], gender fluid[9], and gender neutral[10], which have become major talking points. Surprisingly, trends like men wearing corsets are gaining popularity. This trend seeks to eliminate distinctions between genders completely. While some may accept this simplistically, it raises the paradoxical question of why such efforts to blur gender lines and create confusion about switching between male and female identities are necessary in our time.

What is the Concept of Gender Education?

   The biblical value of sex is not an ambiguous notion where one can be male or female. God created men and women, marking them precisely. However, the spirit of the world (1 Corinthians 2:12) continually raises questions about the next generation through education and culture, politics and laws. Just as God created the universe perfectly, He made every one of us complete as men and women. Being complete in this context does not mean without flaws; instead, it signifies being created perfectly according to God's good purposes.

   The Bible states, "For we are God's workmanship, created in Christ Jesus to do good works, which God prepared in advance for us to do." (Ephesians 2:10). It emphasizes that God, who does not make mistakes (Numbers 23:19), created us as male and female, a noble work of His.

   It is crucial to teach the next generation clearly about this. Instead of emphasizing "gender identity," we should teach them about our "Biblical identity."

The biblical identity education at GCSE is defined as "teaching students to recognize that they were born into the grand plan and hope of the Creator, with a character of joyfulness, as defined by Goodtree Character School." This concept of joyfulness is encapsulated by the phrases "I am precious. You are precious. Therefore, we are happy" and "cultivating the character of a positive attitude by thinking, acting, and speaking in a good way," both as defined by Goodtree Character School.

Particularly, Lesson 3 is titled "Who Are You?" and Lesson 4 is "The Hidden Treasure Within Me." These engaging GCSE stories and activities are designed to help students internalize biblical values regarding their identity and worth.

Distinguishing between "gender identity" and "biblical identity" is significant for several reasons that cannot be taken lightly:

"The thief comes only to steal and kill and destroy; I have come that they may have life, and have it to the full." (John 10:10).

As a woman, my calling and as a man, my calling are profound identities that I cannot choose. Gender is something that can be casually changed based on my feelings or emotions. The arrogance of teaching that biological sex can be changed undermines the healthy physical development of the next generation. This alone inflicts wounds that cannot quickly be healed on the next generation, making it a reason never to take lightly the meaning of gender identity education.

God has commanded blessings towards the next generation: "The Lord bless you and keep you" (Numbers 6:24). Here, "keep" means to watch over, pay close attention to, and preserve as it originally was. It is something to be taken seriously and carelessly handed over. God desires to protect the next generation thoroughly, carefully, and delicately.

God began GCSE (Protecting the beauty of sex through good character), but now the responsibility lies with parents and teachers. In this era, parents and teachers are more crucial than ever to rescue the next generation from the forces of darkness (Ephesians 6:12) that threaten to destroy their precious lives through "Biblical identity education."

6) According to the Oxford English Dictionary, gender is traditionally defined as the state of being male or female, typically with reference to social and cultural differences rather than biological ones. It encompasses the roles, behaviors, activities, and attributes that a given society considers appropriate for men and women.

7) UNESCO's International International technical guidance on sexuality education, 2018 Revision, p. 50, "3.1 The Social Construction of Gender and Gender Norms"

8) Genderless, one of the genders in the Gender Queer, means a person with no gender identity. Namu Wiki

9) A type of genderqueer that changes gender identity fluidly like water or air. Namu Wiki

10) A trend to lead life by eliminating the distinction between men and women. Encyclopedia of Current Affairs

■ Core Themes for Parents and Teachers

Gender Identity Education

Gender education refers to the social and cultural meanings of gender rather than biological sex. It teaches that gender is socially constructed and learned, influencing societal norms of masculinity and femininity.

Biblical Identity Education

My identity is not my choice but a gift from God. From the beginning, there is a marvelous purpose and hope in the Creator's plan for me. Biblical identity celebrates the remarkable providence of God's creation and seeks to express His intended character on Earth fully.

■ Terminology for the Next Generation

Biblical Identity Education :

My identity refers to rejoicing in my gender as it was determined at birth.

■ Learning <Biblical Identity Education> through Good Character

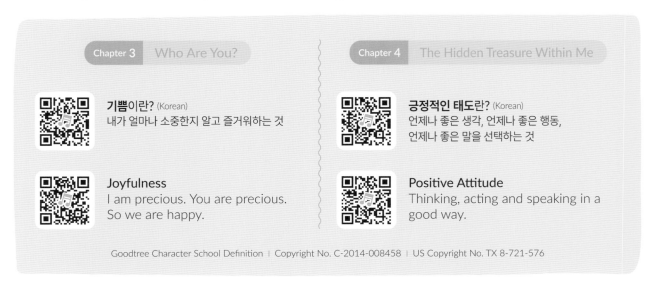

| Chapter 3 | Who Are You? |
| Chapter 4 | The Hidden Treasure Within Me |

기쁨이란? (Korean)
내가 얼마나 소중한지 알고 즐거워하는 것

긍정적인 태도란? (Korean)
언제나 좋은 생각, 언제나 좋은 행동,
언제나 좋은 말을 선택하는 것

Joyfulness
I am precious. You are precious.
So we are happy.

Positive Attitude
Thinking, acting and speaking in a
good way.

Goodtree Character School Definition | Copyright No. C-2014-008458 | US Copyright No. TX 8-721-576

Overview of Good Character Sex Education Plan

	Lesson 3 Who Are You?	Lesson 4 The Hidden Treasure Within Me
GCSE Themes	**Joyfulness** I am precious. You are precious. So we are happy.	**Positive Attitude** Thinking, acting and speaking in a good way.
GCSE Goals	1. Understand that the creator determines one's gender. 2. Recognize one's own worth and take joy in one's gender. 3. Understand the physical structure of males and females and recognize the differences.	1. Acknowledge that one's gender does not change under any circumstances and accept oneself. 2. Understand that one's character stems from one's identity and maintain a positive attitude towards one's gender. 3. Know the differences in gender chromosomes between males and females.
Bible Scriptures	"So God created man in his own image, in the image of God he created him; male and female he created them." (Genesis 1:27)	"For we are God's workmanship, created in Christ Jesus to do good works, which God prepared in advance for us to do." (Ephesians 2:10)
Character Songs	♫ **You Are So Precious** (included in Goodtree Character School Jesus Caby)	♫ **Power Up With Positivity** (included in Goodtree Character School Jesus Caby)
GCSE Activity Names	• **Story Telling** Who Are You? • **Doing & Being** I'm so glad to be a boy (girl)! • **Let's Study** Boys' and Girls' Bodies Are Different (Biological Gender Differences 1 - Physical Structure) • **Building Bridges** Let's Pray Together	• **Story Telling** The Hidden Treasure Within Me • **Doing & Being** I Am Hope • **Let's Study** Understanding Myself! XX, XY (Biological Gender Differences 2 - Sex Chromosomes) • **Building Bridges** Let's Pray Together

* Note: The practical educational activities mentioned above are produced separately in age-specific GCSE workbooks.

Parents and Teachers Learn First!

Do You Know the Woodpecker?

Since 2015, the Goodtree Character School has developed a nature-based character education program that teaches a creative worldview. This program, known as "Creation Character Education in the Forest," focuses on observing various plants and animals in different seasons—spring, summer, fall, and winter—enhancing spiritual growth through a creationist perspective. It is based on twelve patented thematic character traits.

One of the fascinating ecological features highlighted in this program is the woodpecker. Typically, even humans need to make a significant effort to drill a hole in a tree with a sharp tool. However, the woodpecker clings to the tree and drills holes in the trunk with its tiny beak, resembling a skilled artisan. Remarkably, the woodpecker can peck at 20 times per second. The impact force is even more astounding. When comparing the force experienced by an American football player colliding with another player at full speed (about 80g, where g represents gravitational acceleration), the woodpecker's pecking force is significantly higher.

Interestingly, woodpeckers do not suffer from concussions or headaches despite such immense force-the secret lies in the unique structure of their skull and a specialized bone in their tongue.[11] Woodpeckers possess an extraordinary shock-absorbing adaptation that is absent in other birds. Their skull bones' chemical composition and density are distinct, making their skulls harder and more capable of withstanding impact. Moreover, the woodpecker's tongue has a unique bone acting as a spring, significantly minimizing vibrations.

Overlooking Ecological Characteristics in the "Blind Spot" of Gender Equality

What would it be like to ask a woodpecker to talk like a parrot? Or give it webbed feet like a duck simply because it desires them? Or, to break stereotypes, to completely alter the woodpecker's structure so it can do all these things well-is that truly a respectful endeavor?

UNESCO's International Technical Guidance on Sexuality Education teaches respect for others' gender identities without bias.[12] It explicitly states that stereotypes about sexual orientation can lead to gender-based violence (GBV) and, therefore, should be openly challenged.[13]

Some may argue, "What's wrong with gender equality?" or "Why is treating everyone without bias bad?" However, problems often arise in the areas we need to examine more closely.

The gender equality described by UNESCO is not the same as the equality of treating men and women with dignity as we typically understand it. Instead, it demands recognition of all identities labeled as gender, including male while female, female while male, alternate gender, and mixed gender.[14]

For ages 15~18 and above, comprehensive sexuality education (CSE) presents more explicit learning objectives. It teaches that hostility towards homosexuality and gender transition is harmful to those with diverse sexual orientations and gender identities and that everyone should be able to love whomever they wish without discrimination. This is the concept of gender equality emphasized by UNESCO's global trend of CSE.[15]

Consider this: despite biological characteristics, is it an essential global imperative to encourage individuals to change their bodies into male while female, female while male, alternate gender, or mixed gender, just to pursue the gender and love[16] they desire without discrimination?[17] No matter how beautiful something may seem, it can fail if it goes against the order of creation. Males and females have clear responsibilities and roles according to their ecological characteristics.

The Secret of Creating Life: What is Sexual Responsibility ?

Sexual Responsibility is "preserving one's true self with responsibility, cultivating and nurturing one's gender healthily to achieve precious life" (Goodtree Character School Definition).

The third unit of the GCSE curriculum begins with honestly acknowledging one's true self. This means honestly recognizing that humans were created as male or female by the Creator's grand design. Honesty is "winning the trust of others by always telling the truth" (Goodtree Character School Definition). In Lesson 5, students learn through the story "Marriage is Precious" that marriage forms a family through the union of one man and one woman.

Acknowledging all forms of gender, from male to female to an infinite spectrum, is not equality and respect. True sexual responsibility lies in accepting and rejoicing in one's gender as designed by the Creator and preserving one's true self. Our genuine life responsibility is to cultivate and grow our gender beautifully and healthily. Responsibility is "knowing what my tasks are and doing them the best I can" (Goodtree Character School Definition). In Lesson 6, through the story "Men are Fathers, Women are Mothers!" students learn about the responsibility of creating precious life as a male or female.

11) Dr. Sam Van Wassenbergh and his research team at Universiteit Antwerpen in Belgium overturned this conventional wisdom with a study published in 2022 from an evolutionary perspective. They explained that woodpeckers' skulls do not have shock-absorbing structures but have evolved to be optimized for collisions over millions of years. However, the team needed to prove how woodpeckers' brains withstand repeated impacts, presenting a limitation in their claim.

12) UNESCO, International Technical Guidance on Sexuality Education, 2018 Revised Edition, p.50, "3.1 The Social Construction of Gender and Gender Norms"

13) UNESCO, International Technical Guidance on Sexuality Education, 2018 Revised Edition, pp.50-52, "3. Understanding Gender."

14) UNESCO, International Technical Guidance on Sexuality Education, 2018 Revised Edition, pp.112-113, "Glossary," where transgender is defined as male or female, alternate gender, mixed gender, or non-gender.

15) UNESCO, International Technical Guidance on Sexuality Education, 2018 Revised Edition, p.16, "Understanding Comprehensive Sexuality Education."

16) UNESCO, International Technical Guidance on Sexuality Education, 2018 Revised Edition, pp.112-113, "Glossary," where bisexual is defined as a person attracted to more than one gender.

17) UNESCO, International Technical Guidance on Sexuality Education, 2018 Revised Edition, pp.112-113, "Glossary," where transsexual is defined as someone who undergoes medical procedures (including surgery and hormone therapy) to make their body align better with their gender identity.

■ Core Themes for Parents and Teachers

Gender Equality

Recognizing gender queer (third gender) as part of gender. Human society includes individuals who cannot be classified simply as male or female, advocating not only for equality between men and women but also for equality of gender queer individuals and various sexual orientations (bisexuality, pansexuality, homosexuality, etc.).

Sexual Responsibility

Recognizing all forms of gender, including male, female, and third gender, is not equality and respect. It is my responsibility to acknowledge and take joy in my gender as planned by the Creator, who made me male or female. I must preserve my being and nurture my gender to grow healthily.

■ Terminology for the Next Generation

Sexual Responsibility:

Nurturing and growing oneself healthily in order to obtain precious life between one man and one woman.

■ Learning <Sexual Responsibility> through Good Character

| Chapter 5 | Marriage is Precious |

정직이란? (Korean)
어떠한 상황에서도 생각, 말, 행동을 거짓 없이 바르게 표현하여 신뢰를 얻는 것

Honesty
Winning the trust of others by always telling the truth.

| Chapter 6 | Men are Fathers, Women are Mothers! |

책임감이란? (Korean)
내가 해야 할 일이 무엇인지 알고 끝까지 맡아서 잘 수행하는 태도

Responsibility
Knowing what my tasks are and doing them the best I can.

Goodtree Character School Definition | Copyright No. C-2014-008458 | US Copyright No. TX 8-721-576

Overview of Good Character Sex Education Plan

	Lesson 5	Lesson 6
	Marriage is Precious	**Men are Fathers, Women are Mothers!**
GCSE Themes	**Honesty** Winning the trust of others by always telling the truth.	**Responsibility** Knowing what my tasks are and doing them the best I can.
GCSE Goals	1. To express honestly that only males and females exist and to understand the relationships between same-sex and opposite-sex siblings. 2. To realize that marriage forms a family through one man and one woman. 3. To know that life is created through a man's sperm and a woman's egg.	1. To understand the responsibilities that come with being male or female. 2. To protect and keep oneself healthy to fulfill sexual responsibilities. 3. To know the process of becoming a father or mother and to understand the responsibilities of parenthood.
Bible Scriptures	"For this reason a man will leave his father and mother and be united to his wife, and they will become one flesh." (Genesis 2:24)	"Marry and have sons and daughters; find wives for your sons and give your daughters in marriage, so that they too may have sons and daughters. Increase in number there; do not decrease." (Jeremiah 29:6)
Character Songs	♫ Just As You Are (included in Goodtree Character School Jesus Caby)	♫ Renewed Every Morning (included in Goodtree Character School Jesus Caby)
GCSE Activity Names	• **Story Telling** Marriage is Precious • **Doing & Being** Who Will You Marry? • **Let's Study** Sperm + Egg = Me • **Building Bridges** Let's Pray Together	• **Story Telling** Men are Fathers, Women are Mothers! • **Doing & Being** Men and Women, Fathers and Mothers • **Let's Study** A Child Growing in a Woman's Womb • **Building Bridges** Let's Pray Together

* Note: The practical educational activities mentioned above are produced separately in age-specific GCSE workbooks.

GCSE: Good Character Sex Education 63

Parents and Teachers Learn First!

Goodtree Character School What is Possible Through Obedience Education

"Obedience in sex education? Does that make sense?"

I can almost hear the bold questions from smart parents. Even setting aside the 21st century, "in today's world," obedience in sex education seems like an odd combination, doesn't it?

What I can confidently say is that it is only possible through Goodtree Character School's obedience education. Obedience is defined by Goodtree Character School as "following the instructions of others with a good attitude." The core of obedience is knowing who is protecting me. This is precisely where it intersects with biblical sex education.

Teaching about sex should rightfully come from those who protect me. It is not about making decisions on one's own. It is also not about learning from pornography, explicit materials, or peers of similar maturity levels. (We cannot even entrust our children to teachers who have completed comprehensive sex education (CSE)). God has entrusted parents with the protection of the next generation, as stated in "Train a child in the way he should go, and when he is old he will not turn from it" (Proverbs 22:6). Sex education, which deals with life, is a precious worldview that should flow intimately from parents to their children within the family.

Consent Education: The Terrifying Strategy Hidden in Beautiful Words

UNESCO's Comprehensive Sexuality Education (CSE) teaches consent.[18] For children aged 5~8, it starts with emphasizing 'rights over one's body.' This concept is typical of early childhood sex education, where children learn to express their rights over their bodies and how to say "No," "Go away," in uncomfortable situations.

However, as the age increases, the educational content changes. Comprehensive Sexuality Education (CSE) for ages 12~15 emphasizes the right to sexual behavior, teaching that every individual, regardless of sexual orientation, has the right to control their sexual behavior, communicate with partners, and obtain consent. This introduces the concept of 'sexual self-determination,' instilling a humanistic perspective that one's body belongs to oneself.

Suddenly, a question arises. Is it safe to teach children aged 12~15 that they have 'sexual self-determination'? It's challenging to expect mature discernment from most adults, so can we call it education to let the next generation choose whether to endure or not, as if throwing fish to a cat? Moreover, teaching children of this age to actively communicate and seek consent with their sexual partners might seem like learning simple conversation skills, but implicitly, it is almost the same as encouraging sexual relationships at this stage. Who can ultimately protect and take responsibility for the lives of these children? The discomfort remains.

Consent Education: Stripping Parents of Authority

Consent education is a frightening strategy that leads the next generation to redefine their understanding of sex from a humanistic perspective. By emphasizing the freedom of sexual behavior according to sexual orientation, it rejects biblical guidelines, defies traditional values, and creates conflicts with parental upbringing methods. Especially during adolescence, it implies that individuals can choose sexual partners based on their sexual desires, whether heterosexual, homosexual, or bisexual, seemingly focused on alleviating guilt from promiscuous sexual activities.

This type of education conveys the message that one's inherent gender can be chosen at will or changed easily through surgery. The most ironic aspect is that schools and the state directly intervene in significant matters such as changing a child's gender through gender transition protection laws, while parents are left powerless to take any action.

Consent education also clashes with religious values in the same context. By perceiving parental faith education as an oppression of the child's body and emotions, it currently drives healthy spiritual education at home into being labeled as child abuse. It causes children to make all decisions independently, no longer obeying their parents, fundamentally opposing God's creation order and biblical authority. Parents, teachers, and pastors must always be vigilant and cautious about whether this consent education is genuine sex education for the next generation.

According to Lev Semenovich Vygotsky's (1896~1934) scaffolding (cognitive development theory) children need mature adults who teach them a happy life to grow into well-rounded adults. It's the same principle as installing scaffolding during construction to complete the building beautifully and safely.

In the same context, sex education requires the absolute role and protection of parents. Parents must first learn to protect the beauty of sex through good character and be able to discuss sex with their children whenever possible. Consent education strips away this intimate parental authority and teaching, causing potential confusion by suddenly granting 'sexual self-determination' to children who should be learning and growing, leaving them with rights but no responsibilities.

What is Obedience Education?

For the next generation to grow into beautiful adults, they need to go through a period of 'patience' and 'obedience.' In constructing a life, wise education from adults is necessary for a certain period to build one's life with correct thoughts, emotions, and actions. Only those with a healthy worldview can live a happy life.

As the Lord said, "Perseverance must finish its work so that you may be mature and complete, not lacking anything" (James 1:4), GCSE teaches sexuality through obedience education so that the next generation can live a complete life.

In particular, Lesson 7 of GCSE teaches the character of patience, waiting until my body and mind mature. Patience is defined by Goodtree Character School as "waiting in peace for a good thing to happen." Through the GCSE story 'We Need to Wait' and related activities, students practice preparing for beautiful sexuality.

In Lesson 8, 'obedience' rather than 'consent' is taught. The next generation needs obedience education, not consent education. Obedience is defined by Goodtree Character School as "following the instructions of others with a good attitude." Giving 'sexual self-determination' to the growing next generation is as foolish a decision as giving them a weapon unguarded. Through the GCSE story 'The Secret to Protecting Myself,' they learn how to joyfully follow correct instructions and protect themselves.

To build a shining life, good character, which matures by being protected through obedience in daily life, is necessary. Obedience to the directions and teachings of those who protect and love you is what makes a beautiful life flourish.

---

18) UNESCO's International Technical Guidance on Sexuality Education Revised Edition 2018 p.56 '4.2 Consent, Privacy and Bodily Integrity'

■ Core Themes for Parents and Teachers

Consent Education

Consent means clearly expressing my will and recognizing that I am the master of myself. This includes the right to make decisions about my body, implying that if one consents, one can also choose one's gender.

Obedience Education

For a child to grow into a well-rounded adult, mature adults who teach them how to live a happy life are essential. Lev Semenovich Vygotsky (1896-1934) called this scaffolding. Just as scaffolding helps complete a beautiful building, it is the principle that wise adults' education, with correct thoughts, emotions, and actions for a certain period, is necessary to help children construct their lives. It emphasizes that obedience education is more important than consent education as a prerequisite for creating one's life.

■ Terminology for the Next Generation

Protective obedience following the correct instructions of those who protect me until my body and mind grow.

■ Learning <Obedience Education> through Good Character

| Chapter 7 | We Need to Wait |

인내란? (Korean)
좋은 일이 이루어질 때까지 불평 없이 참고 기다리는 것

Patience
Waiting in peace for a good thing to happen.

| Chapter 8 | The Secret to Protecting Myself |

순종이란? (Korean)
나를 보호하고 있는 사람들의 지시에 좋은 태도로 기쁘게 따르는 것

Obedience
Following the instructions of others with a good attitude.

Goodtree Character School Definition | Copyright No. C-2014-008458 | US Copyright No. TX 8-721-576

Overview of Good Character Sex Education Plan

	Lesson 7 We Need to Wait	Lesson 8 The Secret to Protecting Myself
GCSE Themes	Patience Waiting in peace for a good thing to happen.	Obedience Following the instructions of others with a good attitude.
GCSE Goals	1. Wait with patience for the maturity of my body and mind. 2. Understand the physical changes that occur at different ages during human growth.	1. Realize that obeying those who protect me is a way to protect myself. 2. Learn and practice ways to protect myself by gladly following correct instructions.
Bible Scriptures	"Perseverance must finish its work so that you may be mature and complete, not lacking anything." (James 1:4)	"Children, obey your parents in everything, for this pleases the Lord." (Colossians 3:20)
Character Songs	♫ I Persevere With Faith (included in Goodtree Character School Jesus Caby)	♫ I Obey (included in Goodtree Character School Jesus Caby)
GCSE Activity Names	• **Story Telling** We Need to Wait • **Doing & Being** The Healthy and Mature 'Me' • **Let's Study** My Body Has Changed • **Building Bridges** Let's Pray Together	• **Story Telling** The Secret to Protecting Myself • **Doing & Being** Who Protects 'Me'? • **Let's Study** Protecting 'Me' with Correct Instructions • **Building Bridges** Let's Pray Together

* Note: The practical educational activities mentioned above are produced separately in age-specific GCSE workbooks.

Discern the World Through Biblical Sexual Truth
Parents and Teachers Learn First!

The Most Practical Advice from Someone Who Experienced the Greatest Culture

John Dewey, the father of modern education in America, stated, "Education is experience." He believed that experience is more important than anything else in education. The quality of one's life is determined by the experiences they have had.

Here is a person who experienced the most significant culture in human history. He enjoyed the highest levels of wealth, honor, power, and credentials that one could imagine. The era he lived in was so financially prosperous that silver was as common as stones and was not considered a precious metal (1 Kings 10:27). His people had no lack of food and drink (1 Kings 4:20). Diplomatically, his nation maintained peace with all surrounding countries, earning a reputation as a powerful nation (1 Kings 10:21, 31). He composed a thousand and five songs that were more popular than today's world stars (1 Kings 4:32), and people from all over the world flocked to experience this culture annually (1 Kings 10:24~25). This is the story of Solomon, the wisest king in history.

After experiencing all the success, glory, pleasure, and satisfaction, his realistic advice to the next generation is impressive. It is to "Remember your Creator" (Ecclesiastes 12:1). With unparalleled wisdom, he mastered everything. He could do whatever he wanted, yet he taught us the supreme secret of life: to remember the Creator God from one's youth.

Sexuality:
The Secret of 253 Mentions

Looking around at our current times, it is disheartening to see that the next generation lives in a culture that makes it challenging to maintain their faith. Modern culture does not remember the Creator God. Instead, as Audrey Azoulay, Director-General of UNESCO, stated in the foreword of the International Technical Guidance on Sexuality Education, it is rapidly moving towards promoting sexuality to engage the next generation's interest.[19]

Given this trend, the emphasis on the "cultural meaning of gender and sexuality" in UNESCO's International Technical Guidance on Sexuality Education has become more pronounced. It is mentioned 253 times in a document of just 140 pages, highlighting the importance placed on sexuality. Why has sexuality become so urgent and essential?

As previously mentioned, the concept of gender in the Bible is straightforward and clear.[20] There are no complex concepts such as a third gender, intersex, or mixed gender. God created man and woman and gave life through the beautiful gift of gender.

But what changes when we explain this concept of gender using the cultural meaning of sexuality? Viewing gender through the lens of cultural meaning shifts it from being a matter of right and wrong to being accepted as a personal or societal preference. When gender attitudes and forms pass through the filter of "culture," they are presented as free from all norms, moral concepts, conscience, and discernment. This "cultural meaning of gender" becomes a "No touch!" state, making applying any proper standards or criteria difficult.

What is the Biblical sexual truth?

We must remember that gender is a "truth" that engenders and fosters life. Viewing gender as a cultural aspect versus viewing it as a truth presents a significant gap. These fundamentally opposite concepts cannot be reconciled or compromised from beginning to end.

Truth is based on universal and immutable facts. While times change and many philosophical thoughts and values evolve, the principles of life remain constant. God commanded us to "be fruitful and increase" directly linking gender with life.

Thus, the truth about gender, or "biblical sexual truth" is defined as "recognizing gender as a biblical concept that engenders life" (Goodtree Character School Definition). Viewing gender as a series of cultural elements and interpreting it through the lens of sexuality introduces the idea of various genders, including a third gender, that can love one another. Above all, it limits the value of gender to pleasure, ultimately destroying the elements of life by altering the biological characteristics of "me and you."

GCSE (Protecting the beauty of sex through good character) for the Next Generation with Truth

"Do not conform any longer to the pattern of this world, but be transformed by the renewing of your mind. Then you will be able to test and approve what God's will is--his good, pleasing and perfect will" (Romans 12:2)

In the final unit, Unit 5 of the GCSE program, students learn and practice the most beautiful value of humanity-gender-from the perspective of biblical sexual truth. In an era that constantly whispers, "You can do whatever you want. Gender is just a culture," we must teach and dream of the next generation who will protect beautiful gender through the good character trait of self-control.

Self-control is "choosing to do what is right even if it's not what I want" (Goodtree Character School Definition). In Lesson 9, titled "The One Who Overcomes the World," students will have time to remember the self-control of the Creator God.

In Lesson 10, students will learn to discern the times and choose the correct values, protecting beautiful gender with the character trait of wisdom. Wisdom is "using what I have and what I know to help others" (Goodtree Character School Definition). Through the story "True Wisdom," we hope to guide the next generation to the biblical value of gender, leading them to obtain life and have it more abundantly through biblical sexual truth. Educating the next generation to experience the greatness of the Creator who made the world is the most incredible wisdom.

---

19) UNESCO, International Technical Guidance on Sexuality Education, 2018 Revised Edition, p.4 Foreword.

20) Genesis 1:27 - "So God created man in his own image, in the image of God he created him; male and female he created them"

■ Core Themes for Parents and Teachers

Sexuality

Sexuality is fundamental to human life, encompassing physical, psychological, spiritual, social, and cultural aspects. It is a comprehensive concept that includes not only the sexual behaviors of men and women but also emotions, attitudes, norms, understandings, values, and behavioral patterns related to sex. Attitudes and forms of sexuality are defined as 'culture.'

Biblical Sexual Truth

Humans are created as the Lords of all creation. According to the Creator's command to "be fruitful and increase" humans were designed to govern the world, reflecting His image. Therefore, humanity must build a culture guided by a good conscience, universal truths, and values, leading the world. It is not correct to extend the world's culture based on the fundamental principles of sexuality. Sexuality is a means to fulfill the mission to "be fruitful and increase" Expanding a culture that mirrors the Creator's good character is the truth.

■ Terminology for the Next Generation

Biblical Sexual Truth:

Biblical Sexual Truth Finding the meaning of biological sex in the Bible and valuing life highly.

■ Learning <Biblical Sexual Truth> through Good Character

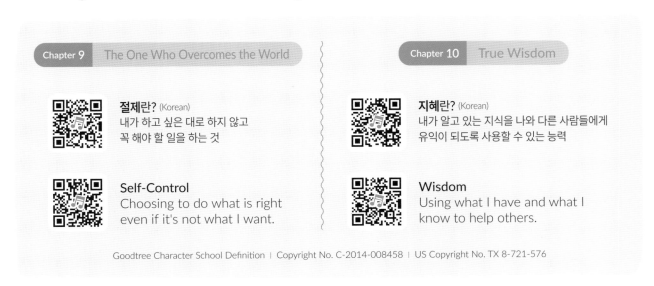

Chapter 9	The One Who Overcomes the World

절제란? (Korean)
내가 하고 싶은 대로 하지 않고 꼭 해야 할 일을 하는 것

Self-Control
Choosing to do what is right even if it's not what I want.

Chapter 10	True Wisdom

지혜란? (Korean)
내가 알고 있는 지식을 나와 다른 사람들에게 유익이 되도록 사용할 수 있는 능력

Wisdom
Using what I have and what I know to help others.

Goodtree Character School Definition | Copyright No. C-2014-008458 | US Copyright No. TX 8-721-576

Overview of Good Character Sex Education Plan

	Lesson 9	Lesson 10
	The One Who Overcomes the World	**True Wisdom**
GCSE Themes	**Self-Control** Choosing to do what is right even if it's not what I want.	**Wisdom** Using what I have and what I know to help others.
GCSE Goals	1. Identify what needs to be controlled to protect my gender. 2. Practice protecting my gender with good character traits, even when it's not what I want to do.	1. Establish correct standards for gender through the wisdom of the Bible. 2. Protect my gender with the truth of the Word and prayer, transforming the world.
Bible Scriptures	"All Scripture is God-breathed and is useful for teaching, rebuking, correcting and training in righteousness, so that the man of God may be thoroughly equipped for every good work" (2 Timothy 3:16~17)	"Above all else, guard your heart, for it is the wellspring of life." (Proverbs 4:23)
Character Songs	🎵 **A Victorious Person** (included in Goodtree Character School Jesus Caby)	🎵 **A Wise Person Is** (included in Goodtree Character School Jesus Caby)
GCSE Activity Names	• **Story Telling** The One Who Overcomes the World • **Doing & Being** Good Character 10 Commandments • **Let's Study** Stop Media to Protect 'Me'! • **Building Bridges** Let's Pray Together	• **Story Telling** True Wisdom • **Doing & Being** Learning Sexual Truth from the Bible • **Let's Study** God's Word Protecting 'Me' • **Building Bridges** Let's Pray Together

* Note: The practical educational activities mentioned above are produced separately in age-specific GCSE workbooks.

Chapter 7

GCSE Counseling Q&A For Parents and Teachers

Parents and teachers who learned GCSE, please answer like this!

1. Early childhood sex education Counseling Q&A

2. Childhood sex education Counseling Q&A

3. Puberty sex education Counseling Q&A

4. Adolescent and adulthood sex education Counseling Q&A

GCSE Counseling Q&A for Parents and Teachers

Biblical Sex Education helps shape a proper Christian worldview, enriching life. Just as children's cognitive abilities are activated, and concepts are established through questions, 'sex education' also shapes a child's 'sexual identity' through age-appropriate questions. When young children ask questions about sex, if parents and teachers provide the correct answers from a biblical perspective, the next generation will have the power to design their lives beautifully.

'GCSE Counseling Q&A for Parents and Teachers' provides answers based on 'biblical sex education' to the questions about sex that parents and teachers face. Engaging with the next generation in questions and answers about 'sex' is another form of 'character dialogue method,' aiming to form 'beautiful relationships with children.'

Parents and teachers must first learn and equip themselves with 'biblical sex education.' Rejecting humanistic sex education that undermines the order and authority of the Creator who made sex and finding answers from the Bible can help protect children's lives and enable them to live abundant lives. Providing answers through biblical sex education will be an essential opportunity for the next generation to build a framework of a Christian worldview within themselves.

💙 Practical guide for GCSE (Protecting the beauty of sex through good character) can be conducted with age-specific GCSE workbooks.

Early Childhood Sex Education Counseling Q&A

Early Childhood Q1. My child in kindergarten engages in masturbation.

When a boy fiddles with his genitals or a girl rubs her genitals, parents often struggle with whether to scold the child or ignore the behavior. Sometimes, they might even leave the situation. Instead of reacting alarmingly, kindly ask, "What are you doing now? Can you explain it to me?" Early childhood is a time when children become very curious about their gender and their bodies. It's important not to view this curiosity as inherently dirty or prematurely label it as masturbation. Children might engage in these behaviors because they feel itchy or uncomfortable due to their underwear. Listen to your child's response and explain naturally.

Say something like, "This part of your body is very precious and was wonderfully made by God. It is susceptible and important. If you touch it with dirty hands, it can hurt or become painful. Since it's such a special part of your body, you shouldn't touch it just anywhere and not let anyone else touch it. It's a significant place from which babies come, and you must take care of it until you grow up to be a mom or dad."

Ensure the conversation is comfortable and natural so your child doesn't feel unnecessary guilt. Start an honest dialogue with your child instead of fearing or avoiding the behavior. If cleanliness is an issue, encourage your child to wash up and change their underwear: "Let's clean up and change your underwear. Right now, I'll help you because you're young, but later, you'll need to clean this precious part of your body by yourself and ensure no one else touches it."

Begin incorporating sex education naturally through teaching your child about body care. Explain that God has intricately created us and that this particular part of our bodies, capable of giving life, needs to be cherished and cared for from an early age. Providing alternative activities to engage their senses can also be effective. Use various toys to encourage hand play. Remember, biblical sex education involves inviting the Creator, who made our bodies into the conversation from an early age.

Q2. When should sex education begin?

Sex education should start from the moment a child is born. During infancy, using everyday language such as "Let's have some milk from mommy" or "Oh! You got pee on your penis" helps to teach children to cherish their bodies, which is the beginning of sex education. After age 5, children's curiosity and questions increase, prompting parents to consider 'early childhood sex education' more seriously.

The key is to instill biblical sexual values according to the child's developmental stage. Some illustrated books based on Comprehensive Sexuality Education (CSE) have faced strong opposition from parents for showing explicit images of parents having sex or displaying naked bodies and genitals under the guise of addressing children's curiosity. While some argue that children should be taught the correct terms for reproductive organs like the vagina, clitoris, and testicles to prevent sexual abuse, there is concern that early exposure to sexual content may lead to premature sexualization.

As the British poet Byron said, "Words are thoughts. When a tiny drop of ink touches the mind like mist, hundreds and thousands of thoughts branch out." Teaching children the detailed names and functions of reproductive organs is not sex education. Instead, explain the purpose of creating males and females, the unchanging principles of gender (such as chromosomes), and the preciousness of life. Begin by teaching about our bodies with the Creator's name, helping children understand His plan and thoughts about their bodies.

Q3. Is it okay for a father and daughter or a brother and sister to bathe together?

When children are between 0 and 3 years old, bathing with an opposite-gender parent or sibling can be an opportunity to observe, understand, and explore the physical differences between genders. However, around age 5, when children become more sensitive to gender and aware of their bodies, it is advisable to start separate baths. From this stage, it is generally better for a same-gender parent to take care of the child's bathing needs as children begin to develop a more sensitive and thoughtful attitude towards their bodies. Special Considerations for Blended Families: In blended families, it is essential to adhere to the principle of not having opposite-gender parents bathe opposite-gender children or opposite-gender siblings bathe together from the start. Prevention is wiser than addressing issues after they arise.

Q4. My child keeps asking how babies are made. How should I answer?

When your child asks, "How are babies made?" it's an excellent opportunity to introduce sex education naturally. You can explain it like this:

"Among all the things God created, human beings are the most precious and valuable. Every person starts as a baby. God planned for babies to be born when a man and a woman come together in love. He placed the seeds to create a baby inside a man and a woman's body, which becomes active as their bodies grow into adulthood. So, we must wait until our bodies mature into adulthood.

When the right time comes, and a man and a woman get married and love each other, the baby seed in the man, called sperm, meets the baby seed in the woman, called an egg. This is how a baby is created. The sperm and egg meet and become one, and the baby grows in the mother's womb, like a house for the baby. After about nine months, a beautiful baby is born from the mother's belly. That day is the baby's birthday. Babies are made from the love of their parents, which is why beautiful people like you are born!"

If your child asks for more details, you can say, "There is a special way that the sperm and egg meet, which I will explain more when you are older." Avoid giving fantastical explanations like "The baby was dropped from the sky." Instead, teach your child about the Creator's plan and providence in creating life from an early age.

Childhood Sex Education Counseling Q&A

 Q1. What should I do if my child witnesses the parents having sex?

Do not scold or avoid the situation. Instead, ask the child, "What did you see?" and "How did it make you feel?" This will help you understand exactly what the child saw. Children might think the father is hurting the mother, that they are fighting, or they might mistake it for wrestling.

You can explain, "I see. But actually, mommy and daddy were showing love to each other. The way married couples show love is different from how you play. You will understand this more when you grow up."

If the child is shocked and avoids the parents, say, "Mommy and daddy were showing love. What you saw is something only adults do. We should have locked the door, so it was our mistake, not yours." Make sure to explain that there is a unique way for parents to show love that children should not see, and it was an accident they did.

 Q2. What should I do if my child is exposed to pornography?

As secondary sexual characteristics begin to develop, curiosity about sex significantly increases, and individuals are indirectly or directly exposed to sexual information. During this period, there is a possibility of exposure to pornography. Comprehensive Sex Education (CSE) often treats 'sexual experiences' as a form of enjoyable play or light amusement, which hinders the next generation from developing proper sexual values. This approach contributes to an increased likelihood of the next generation being indirectly exposed to sexual experiences and sexuality. As influential figures in the lives of young people, it's our role to shape a sexual culture that doesn't treat sex as an outlet for self-gratification or a personal preference, which could lower the age at which sexual experiences occur.

Parents must provide accurate sex education to children exposed to pornography. Pornographic content can be shocking and may lead children to try and imitate what they see, potentially resulting in inappropriate or harmful behavior. Ask your child what they felt and thought while watching the video. Explain that pornography does not depict normal sexual behavior. It is often exaggerated, much like actors performing in a movie. Inform them that marital sex is different, based on mutual love, respect, and God's blessing.

Teach your child that sex is a beautiful act created by God for a man and woman, particularly within marriage, to express love and create life. Explain that because sex is beautiful according to the character of God, it is essential to wait until they are mature and responsible enough to handle its consequences appropriately.

 ## Q3. How should I guide my child in opposite-gender relationships?

The next generation grows through relationships. The framework of human relationships, beginning with the parent-child relationship, sets the basic relationship structure for life. From infancy, the attachment formed with caregivers, especially the mother, influences the fundamental trust versus mistrust in relationships and social interactions.

By age 2.5, children develop social skills and the need for friends, primarily forming social relationships with same-gender friends. As they go through puberty, they become aware of their sexuality and develop curiosity about the opposite gender. Opposite-gender relationships are a natural part of growing into adulthood. During childhood and adolescence, broad friendship experiences prepare children for future romantic relationships. Healthy romantic experiences lead to the forming of mature interpersonal relationships that can contribute to a happy family life.

Good character traits are essential for developing relationships, including opposite-gender relationships. Important characteristics include attentiveness, caring, gratefulness, joyfulness, self-control and responsibility, patience and honesty, creativity and wisdom, and a positive attitude and obedience. Teaching the next generation these qualities helps them respect and consider others, communicate effectively, and move beyond selfishness. Character education is vital for forming respectful and mature relationships with the opposite gender.

Rather than rushing into opposite-gender relationships, encourage children to set significant goals and understand that developing good character prepares them for healthy relationships. Explain to anxious children that their current efforts in practicing good character prepare them for future relationships.

 ### Q4. How should I explain nocturnal emissions and menstruation to my child?

As puberty begins, hormones cause changes in the body. Boys start preparing to become fathers, and girls start preparing to become mothers. This is why they experience nocturnal emissions and menstruation. Explain these changes kindly and in detail.

For boys, say, "Nocturnal emissions are when a slippery liquid comes out while you sleep without knowing. This is not bad. It means you are becoming a healthy man and preparing to be a father. Tell dad (or mom) when this happens, and we will congratulate you. Your body is getting ready for the possibility of fatherhood in the future. But since you are not yet socially or economically responsible, you must wait until ready. Having sex involves emotional and physical connections, so doing it before you are ready can hurt both people involved."

For girls, explain, "During puberty, female hormones become active, and your body starts changing into a woman's body. Menstruation starts this process, indicating that you can eventually become a mother. These changes should not be treated with embarrassment but celebrated as you are becoming an adult. Consider planning a 'GCSE Party' to celebrate this milestone with your family, making it a joyful and proud occasion."

Puberty Sex Education GCSE Counseling Q&A

 Q1. How far can physical contact go in a romantic relationship?

Physical contact is a means of communication. A mother can warmly hug her son, and a father can wrap his arm around his daughter's shoulder to express love. Physical contact between boys and girls can also express intimate feelings toward each other. However, since adolescents have difficulty exercising self-control, it is wise to set boundaries for physical contact between the sexes. This principle applies even in adulthood. It is crucial to respect each other and stop physical contact that the other person does not want. Mainly, sexual intercourse is a precious gift that God has permitted within marriage, so it should be enjoyed after marriage.

In a romantic relationship, focusing on activities that provide emotional and psychological satisfaction rather than physical contact is important. Explain that engaging in sexual relations without fully understanding each other can damage the respect and care in the relationship. Encourage your children to practice wise actions that enhance their self-esteem and emphasize that sexual intercourse can lead to unintended pregnancies, which can be a threat to new life.

 Q2. What should I do if my child is addicted to Social Media Pornography, porn, or drugs?

In the past, children addicted to pornography, porn, or drugs were often treated with medication or therapy. However, now we need to think about "How can we recover a child with an addicted brain?" Modern neuroscientists emphasize self-control, or "good character," as the most crucial key to overcoming addiction. Dr. Anna Lembke, a psychiatrist at Stanford University and head of an addiction treatment center, explains in her book "Dopamine Nation"

(2022)[21] the mechanisms of dopamine and addiction. Dopamine is a major neurotransmitter involved in pleasure, reward, and motivation. Exposure to SNS pornography, porn, or drugs causes a rapid increase in dopamine levels, leading to a so-called "dopamine spike" and a sense of pleasure.

However, the problem arises after this "high dopamine reward." To maintain a balance between pleasure and pain, the brain enters a "dopamine deficit state" after the peak of pleasure, causing a rapid drop in dopamine levels. As a result, the brain requires more, more robust, and more prolonged stimuli to achieve the same pleasure, leading to chronic dopamine deficiency and addiction. In this state, the brain's normal function to uphold human beliefs and values deteriorates, increasingly leaning towards "animalistic instincts" over good thoughts, emotions, and actions.

According to a survey by South Korea's Ministry of the Interior and Safety, students exposed to pornography often perceive perverted scenes as natural (16.5%), view their peers as sexual objects (7.9%), and feel urges for sexual harassment or assault (5%). Additionally, exposure to pornographic content can easily lead to inappropriate behaviors such as explicit chatting, sending lewd texts or photos, voyeurism, and pseudo-sexual acts.[22]

Misguided sex education, implemented under the guise of guaranteeing human freedom, teaches that sexual desires can be fulfilled anytime, with anyone, or even alone if one desires. However, such education results in excessive dopamine release, damaging children's brains. Brain scans clearly show the difference: healthy brains have well-functioning dopamine transmission and activation, while addicted brains show reduced activation and chronic dopamine deficiency.

Neuroscientists indicate that for an addicted brain to return to its original state, at least four weeks of "abstinence from addiction" are necessary. However, a frightening fact is that even if the brain returns to its original state, it retains the memory of the addiction for life. In other words, even if one makes a concerted effort to revert to a pre-addiction state from SNS pornography, drugs, and so on, after more than four weeks, the frightening possibility of relapse looms large if one is exposed to the same situation even once.

Therefore, in a situation where large or small addictions are damaging a child's brain, how can one fundamentally overcome and recover from addiction? Neuroscientists unanimously emphasize self-control, i.e., cutting off the stimuli and maintaining that state. They explain that practicing the 'good character' of self-control is a more effective way to revert an addicted brain than drugs or psychological treatment.

Self-control is choosing to do what is right even if it's not what I want (Goodtree Character School Definition). Teach your children the mechanism of self-control and the brain. Without practicing self-control, the problem of addiction cannot be fundamentally resolved.

The age at which children first encounter pornography is becoming younger. They start watching pornography in the 4th to 6th grade (48.7%)[23]. Studies show that children exposed to pornography in elementary school use it more when they become high school students.[24] Therefore, it is crucial to inform your children that the more freely they indulge in SNS pornography, drugs, etc., the more their brain gets damaged, and the more they practice self-control though GCSE from a young age, the healthier their brains will be. The good character of self-control restores your child's addicted brain.

for Puberty ⭐ **Q3. I caught my son masturbating. How should I react?**

When you catch your child masturbating, take a moment to apologize first. Say, "Oh! Sorry, I didn't know. You need some alone time, too. But you should lock the door if you need privacy!" Handle it naturally and with humor. The issue might become more secretive if parents react with shock and seriousness.

If the appropriate ways to respond to hormones are not learned during the growing process, it can become a sensitive issue that could lead to sexual violence. Discuss and understand sexual hormones and how to react to them naturally. Exercise is also an excellent method. Your child needs not parental shock and scolding but practice expressing and controlling thoughts, emotions, and behaviors according to good character and sexual values.

Have a comfortable conversation with your child. Say, "○○you must have been surprised, right? Mom was surprised, too. You are now at an age where you are becoming aware of sexual pleasure. We need to talk about sex as well. Sex is not something that is made to be expressed or used freely at our whim. When you get married, your spouse will be the one to awaken your sexuality for the first time, making it the most meaningful, enjoyable, and stable. However, if we use sexual energy according to our selfish desires, the feelings or pleasure of sex can be damaged. You might seek stronger stimuli, but it won't be satisfying. Trying to relieve it through methods like masturbation, pornography, prostitution, or one-night stands may feel good temporarily, but eventually, sex becomes dull and empty. People are structured in a way that sharing sex with a spouse through marriage is the most enjoyable and valuable. Sexual desire is not just a craving for sex but an energy for creating life. Let's find healthy ways to release sexual desire. Exercise is also a good method."

Reference: Discuss the topics covered by Dr. Anna Lembke, a psychiatrist and professor at Stanford University School of Medicine, in her book 'Dopamine Nation' (2022) or by Professor Gary Wilson, who researched the harms of pornography in his book 'Your Brain on Porn' (2023). Talk to your child about the impact of the character trait of self-control on our brain.

for Puberty ⭐ Q4. I found condoms in my child's bag. What should I do?

There was an incident in American schools where 4th and 5th-grade students were taught sex education, with female students putting condoms on a male model's erect penis, which received many complaints from parents. The school, however, stated that it was a legally conducted lesson for the students' sex education.

Moreover, in Chicago, the Board of Education announced that condoms would be available for students from 5th grade and above in elementary, middle, and high schools, which received many complaints from parents. The Board of Education officials argued that they need to be accessible for their own and others' health. However, parents protested that such education for children aged 10-12 would only stimulate curiosity and encourage irresponsible sexual behavior. (Yonhap News, July 8, 2021. "Providing Condoms in Schools for 5th Graders? American Parents Outraged.")

In South Korea, there was also an incident at a high school in Jeollanam-do where they planned to conduct sex education by putting condoms on bananas, but it was canceled due to parental protests. (Hankyoreh Newspaper, July 13, 2020. "Condom Practice Canceled Due to Parental Opposition: Jeonnam Office of Education Says It Was Appropriate...")

Schools insist on condom education to prevent unwanted pregnancies, sexually transmitted diseases, and AIDS. However, as many parents fear, such education may stimulate young children's sexual curiosity, leading to reckless sexual play. As comprehensive sex education (CSE) based on UNESCO's "International Technical Guidance on Sexuality Education (2018 revised edition)" is implemented in schools, there have been continuous reports of excessive sexual problems among teenagers. Issues like frequent mention of abortion involvement in or exposure to online sexual crimes are rapidly increasing. The "Gyeonggi Province Student Human Rights Ordinance," which accepted CSE, includes unimaginable provisions such as the right for teenagers to have sex and the right to attend school while pregnant, all under the guise of human rights, causing serious concerns and side effects.

It is doubtful whether such education, tailored to the developmental stages of different age groups, has justifiable reasons and effective outcomes for teenagers. Adolescence is when individuals should strive to establish their identity and work towards their dreams for the future. Sex education that views the body as a material object and promotes pleasure and play, under the name of humanistic sex education, needs careful review from the goals to the content. Instead of the sex above education, teenagers urgently need biblical sex education that makes them realize the Creator's unique plan and mission for their lives and helps them envision and prepare their lives as beautiful legacies of God (Ephesians 1:1~3).

---

21) Anna Lembke (2022). "Dopamine Nation". Flow Publishing.

22) Ministry of Public Administration and Security (2012). "5% of Youth Who Watched Pornography Felt Impulses for Sexual Assault or Rape" - Results of a Survey on Youth Use of Adult Materials. Ministry of Public Administration and Security.

23) Kim Hye-ja, Sim Mi-jeong (2014). "The Influence of Adolescent Exposure to Internet Pornography on Sexual Awareness and Attitudes towards Dating". Journal of Digital Convergence Research, 12(5), 367-376.

24) Sim Jae-woong (2010). "The Influence of the Timing of Adolescent Exposure to Pornography on Attitudes Towards Pornography". Korean Association for Women's Communication Studies, Media, Gender & Culture, 16, 75-104.

Instead of provocative sex education like "putting on condoms," I am convinced that practicing sex education with biblical sensitivity towards sexuality, biblical identity, sexual responsibility, obedience to the biblical sexual order, and maintaining sexual truth-what I propose as "GCSE"-will be safer and more precious for the next generation.

Adolescent and Adulthood Sex Education GCSE Counseling Q&A

 **Q1. How should I deal with a friend who is homosexual?**

While conducting a "Good Character Seminar" in California, I received many consultation notes from parents. Surprisingly, many of them were about how to handle the situation when their child's college roommate is homosexual. Even in families of pastors who have served in church ministry their whole lives, there were instances where the child, upon turning 18, came out as homosexual, shocking the parents.

The issue of "homosexuality" is now a close and personal matter for many of us. Especially in countries and regions where the "Anti-Discrimination Act" has been passed, reverse discrimination phenomena occur, protecting homosexuals and imposing disadvantages for so-called "hate speech," making it difficult to speak out.

The "International Technical Guidance on Sexuality Education (revised 2018)," disseminated worldwide, comprises a spiral curriculum with meticulous and repetitive core goals for ages 5 to 18, aiming to change the sexual values of the next generation. It is nearly impossible for parents to reverse the sexual values of children who have thoroughly received comprehensive sexuality education (CSE) until the age of 18.

Moreover, CSE connects sex education with human rights education, presenting opposition to and suppression of one's preferences as "power groups" to be countered. Therefore, the next generation, having received this education, will not hesitate to oppose any resistance to their sexual preferences, even from their parents. This is very dangerous.

Thus, the best thing parents can do is to teach their children "biblical values" regarding sex education from a young age. Do not forget! Sex education is an essential form of "values education."

To successfully carry out this values and worldview education, parents and children must maintain a "close relationship." People tend to listen to those they like and follow the values of those they are close to. One feature of CSE is that it is implemented in schools without providing detailed information to parents at home. Busy parents who leave the education of their children entirely to schools may find themselves facing an unexpected personality in their 18-year-old children.

To prevent this, parents should:

Start "biblical values-based sex education" early.

Closely observe and maintain an intimate relationship with their children as they grow.

They frequently discuss their faith and values with their growing children so that the children adopt biblical values themselves.

Demonstrate a loving and robust parent-child relationship.

Ensure that time spent with parents is enjoyable and safe.

Frequently travel together to foster family unity.

By 18, individuals have a strong will to build their own lives. The goal of sex education should be set in advance so that they can choose better values by their own decision, not by coercion.

Q2. What should I do if my child has an aversion to the opposite sex?

Comprehensive Sexuality Education (CSE) enhances "gender sensitivity." It teaches how to find and oppose experiences of disadvantage due to gender sensitively. This practice naturally leads to a feeling of aversion towards the opposite sex.

However, the sex education advocated by GCSE aims for "Biblical Sensitivity." It teaches the good character of sensitively and delicately seeking the Creator's providence and plan. The plan and providence of God, who created male and female, are to be met with gratitude and joy. God, who created man, said, "Be fruitful and increase in number and fill the earth" Man's existence is a call to be the "ruler of all creatures," resembling the image of God, the Creator of life. He was given the gift of dominion.

However, it was not good for man to be alone. God created a woman and called her "Ezer Kenegdo." "Kenegdo" means "alongside," and "Ezer" means "a life-giver." The woman is significant as a being who gives life to the man alongside him. The union and harmony of men and women filling the earth is the providence of the Creator. It is a beautiful blessing of a relationship that resembles the image of the Creator through "togetherness." To achieve this, we must start proper sex education that respects each other and is grateful for their existence.

Q3. How should I explain dating, marriage, and cohabitation?

Love comes with responsibility. The world's view that seeks convenience without taking responsibility and wanting benefits without bearing losses is shaking the modern concept of marriage. Cohabitation without marriage and cohabiting before marriage is prevalent. Among young college students, some couples easily live together under the pretext of sharing rent and saving living expenses. However, true love is a respectful and responsible relationship.

Trying to live easily according to worldly values can leave indelible scars on the body and mind. God's values are that beloved children live beautifully preserved on this earth and be delivered from temptations and trials. Parents should be role models at home so the next generation learns to love rightly.

Praying for a pious life over convenience and educating about the blessing of child-rearing through the fruit of love in marriage is urgently needed.

Q4. How should I speak to a child who has been sexually assaulted?

Love without respect becomes violence. Sex education that does not teach respect can make our children either victims or perpetrators. Forced sexual intercourse that the other party does not want is a violent injury. A person who has been sexually assaulted feels that their life is shattered and over. While it is undeniable that sexual violence is devastating, it is hopeful that it is not everything in life. Life is not composed solely of sex; it is a holistic existence. We must tell them that even if their sexuality is damaged, it does not mean their entire life is ruined and that their life is still bright and beautiful.

Also, make it clear that it is not the fault of the person who was assaulted but that the person who committed the violence is at fault. Tell your child, "We still love you. Nothing has changed because of this. You are still precious." If the child becomes pregnant because of this incident, let them choose about their life. It is not something parents can force. Parents should respect and support their child's decision. If there are parents who comfort and support their child's heart through more conversations and solve life's problems together, the child will regain strength and live a brilliant life again.

Chapter 8

Glossary of GCSE Terms

- Glossary of GCSE Terms & Definitions of 12 Good Character Traits by Goodtree Character School
- Glossary of Terms from UNESCO's International Technical Guidance on Sexuality Education

Glossary of GCSE Terms

CHAPTER 1

Biblical Sensitivity

Biblical sensitivity education cultivates the sensitivity to find the truths of the biblical worldview in daily life. Contrary to the gender sensitivity taught by the world, it involves finding the creative principles of the Creator in everyday life and discovering the grand plan and mission hidden in our wonderfully created bodies and genders, striving to emulate the character of the Creator.

Good Character |

Creativity: Trying different ways with new ideas.

Caring: Giving love and attention to the world around me.

CHAPTER 2

Biblical Identity Education

My identity is not my choice but a gift from God. The Creator has had a great plan and hope for me since the beginning. Biblical identity education helps me rejoice in my existence, created in the image of the Creator, and fully express my character on this earth according to His hope.

Good Character |

Joyfulness: I am precious. You are precious. So we are happy.

Positive Attitude: Thinking, acting and speaking in a good way.

CHAPTER 3

Sexual Responsibility

Recognizing all forms of gender, including male, female, and third gender, is not equality and respect. It is my responsibility to acknowledge and take joy in my gender as planned by the Creator, who made me male or female. I must preserve my being and nurture my gender to grow healthily.

Good Character |

Honesty: Winning the trust of others by always telling the truth.

Responsibility: Knowing what my tasks are and doing them the best I can.

CHAPTER 4
Obedience Education

For a child to grow into a well-rounded adult, mature adults who teach them how to live a happy life are essential. Lev Semenovich Vygotsky (1896-1934) called this scaffolding. Just as scaffolding helps complete a beautiful building, it is the principle that wise adults' education, with correct thoughts, emotions, and actions for a certain period, is necessary to help children construct their lives. It emphasizes that obedience education is more important than consent education as a prerequisite for creating one's life.

Good Character |

Patience: Waiting in peace for a good thing to happen.

Obedience: Following the instructions of others with a good attitude.

CHAPTER 5
Biblical Sexual Truth

Humans are created as the rulers of all creatures, following the Creator's command to "be fruitful and increase." Therefore, expanding the culture of this world based on fundamental sexual principles is not correct. Sexuality is a pathway to fulfill the mission of "being fruitful and multiplying." Expanding a happy culture resembling the Creator's good character is the truth.

Good Character |

Wisdom: Using what I have and what I know to help others.

Self-Control: Choosing to do what is right even if it's not what I want.

Sources:

- Lee Young Suk (2005). Character Education Guide for Parents and Teachers: Attentiveness. Seoul: Beautiful Fruit.
- Lee Young Suk (2007). Now It's Character. Seoul: Beautiful Fruit.
- Lee Young Suk (2014). Korean 12 Character Education Theory. Seoul: Goodtree Character School.
- Lee Young Suk (2016). 12 Character Theory. Sigma Press.

Glossary of Terms from UNESCO's International Technical Guidance on Sexuality Education∗

Gender Sensitivity

Gender sensitivity education aims to cultivate 'gender sensitivity,' the sensitivity to detect elements of gender discrimination in daily life. It is an education that understands each other's diversity and aims to realize a society where everyone is respected and treated equally.

Gender Education
(Gender Identity Education)

Gender education refers to the social and cultural meanings of gender rather than biological sex. It teaches that gender is socially constructed and learned, influencing societal norms of masculinity and femininity.

Gender Equality

Recognizing gender queer (third gender) as part of gender. Human society includes individuals who cannot be classified simply as male or female, advocating not only for equality between men and women but also for equality of gender queer individuals and various sexual orientations (bisexuality, pansexuality, homosexuality, etc.).

Consent Education

Consent means clearly expressing my will and recognizing that I am the master of myself. This includes the right to make decisions about my body, implying that if one consents, one can also choose one's gender.

sexuality

Sexuality is fundamental to human life, encompassing physical, psychological, spiritual, social, and cultural aspects. It is a comprehensive concept that includes not only the sexual behaviors of men and women but also emotions, attitudes, norms, understandings, values, and behavioral patterns related to sex. Attitudes and forms of sexuality are defined as 'culture.'

Gay*

: A person who is primarily attracted to and/or has relationships with someone of the same gender. Commonly used for men, some women also use this term.

Gender*

: Refers to the social attributes and opportunities associated with being male and female and the relationships between women and men and girls and boys, as well as the relations between women and those between men. These attributes, opportunities and relationships are socially constructed and are learned through socialization processes.

Gender identity*

: a person's deeply felt internal and individual experience of gender, which may or may not correspond with the sex assigned to them at birth. This includes the personal sense of the body which may involve, if freely chosen, modification of bodily appearance or function (by medical, surgical or other means)

Gender non-conformity / conforming*
: people who do not conform to either of the binary gender definitions of male or female, as well as those whose gender expression may differ from standard gender norms. In some instances, individuals are perceived by society as gender nonconforming because of their gender expression. However, these individuals may not perceive themselves as gender nonconforming. Gender expression and gender non-conformity are clearly related to individual and social perceptions of masculinity and femininity.

Gender variance*
: expressions of gender that do not match those predicted by one's assigned sex at birth.

Gender-based violence*
: violence against someone based on gender discrimination, gender role expectations and/or gender stereotypes; or based on the differential power status linked to gender that results in, or is likely to result in, physical, sexual or psychological harm or suffering.

Inclusive education*
: the process of strengthening the capacity of the education system to reach out to all learners.

Intersex*
: people who are born with sex characteristics (including genitals, gonads and chromosome patterns) that do not fit typical binary notions of male or female bodies. 'Intersex' is an umbrella term used to describe a wide range of natural bodily variations. In some cases, intersex traits are visible at birth, while in others they are not apparent until puberty. Some chromosomal intersex variations may not be physically apparent at all. Being intersex relates to biological sex characteristics and is distinct from a person's sexual orientation or gender identity. An intersex person may be straight, gay, lesbian or bisexual, and may identify as female, male, both or neither.

Sexual orientation*
: Each person's capacity for profound emotional, affectional, and sexual attraction to, and intimate and sexual relations with, individuals of a different gender (heterosexual) or the same gender (homosexual) or more than one gender (bisexual or pansexual).

Transsexual*
: The term 'transsexual' is sometimes used to describe transgender people who have undergone or want to undergo medical procedures (which may include surgical and hormonal treatment) to make their body more congruent with their gender identity.

Sources:

- UNESCO's International Technical Guidance on Sexuality Education (2018 Revised Edition)

Conclusion

Quietly and Subtly!

I heard a song by a male duet on YouTube. The melody was sweet, but the lyrics were chilling. The title of the song is "We'll Convert Your Children." Let's look at the lyrics:

> "We'll convert your children.
> Happens bit by bit
> quietly and subtly!
> And you will barely notice it.
> You (parents) can keep'em from disco
> warn about San Francisco (the stronghold of homosexuality)
> make'em wear pleated pants.
> We don't care.
> We'll convert your children.
> We'll make them tolerant and fair."

This is a song with a terrifying strategy aimed at the next generation. It quietly and subtly undermines biblical sexual values through a cultural approach. Culture is the sum of human knowledge, beliefs, and behaviors. By changing the concept of "sex," they aim to overturn and shake the very foundation of our lives, swallowing up the remarkable heritage of humanity in culture, art, education, politics, and science that has been preserved so far.

As awake parents and teachers, it is time for us to start a revolution. To save the lives of the next generation, parents, teachers, schools, churches, political leaders, and spiritual leaders must unite and launch a quiet and subtle strategy to save the next generation starting now.

For a long time, the strategy has been to secretly infiltrate the education field for ages 5~18 with anti-biblical language and concepts in the "sex education" curriculum globally. Now it is time to block this and urgently implement biblical sex education. The strategy must unfold to restore the image of God in the next generation.

I have systematized the "GCSE" to protect beautiful sex with good character. Character expresses a person's thoughts, emotions, and actions (Young Suk Lee, 2005). The expression of thoughts, emotions, and actions is part of culture. Just as each country and family has a unique culture, the principles of forming character and culture are the same. They are also similar in leading to the worldview and values that determine life. Depending on one's interpretative system based on culture, the conditions for experiencing emotions, the types, frequency, and intensity of experienced emotions differ (Markus & Kitayama, 1991).

Parents of faith must allow the next generation to experience the Bible from a young age so they can set an unwavering identity flag. "Good character" is God's character found in the Bible. That is why "good character" is an unchanging truth. I dream of a world where the next generation understands, uses, and rejoices in sexuality according to the thoughts, emotions, and actions of the One who made the world and started sex. I hope the "GCSE" culture spreads globally and the sea of life governed by the King of Peace waves to all nations. Let's continue singing the song "GCSE" together so that the beautiful world created by God waves to the nations.

August 2024,
Young Suk Lee, Ph.D.